LEARN

Arabic

WORDS

head
رأس
(ra's)

vegetables
خضروات
(khaDrawaat)

hand
يد
(yad)

body
جسم
(jism)

fruit
فاكهة
(faakihah)

BY M. J. YORK • ILLUSTRATED BY KATHLEEN PETELINSEK

The Child's World®
childsworld.com

Published by The Child's World®
1980 Lookout Drive • Mankato, MN 56003-1705
800-599-READ • www.childsworld.com

Acknowledgments
Translator: Mohammed Adel Hussein,
Arabic Langauge Teaching Specialist, University of Minnesota

ISBN 9781503835795
LCCN 2019944711

Printed in the United States of America

ABOUT THE AUTHOR

M. J. York is a children's author and
editor living in Minnesota. She loves
learning about different people
and places.

ABOUT THE ILLUSTRATOR

Kathleen Petelinsek loves to draw
and paint. She also loves to travel
to exotic countries where people
speak foreign languages. She lives
in Minnesota with her husband, two
dogs, and a fluffy cat.

CONTENTS

Introduction to Arabic

About 315 million people speak Arabic as their first language. Many Arabic speakers live in North Africa, the Arabian Peninsula, and the Middle East. It is the language of Islam and its holy book, the Koran. Arabic is related to Hebrew and many other languages of Africa and the Middle East. It is written from right to left.

There are 28 letters in Modern Standard Arabic. Not all Arabic sounds can be represented in English letters. Capital letters represent these sounds. Most words in this book are Modern Standard Arabic. Some words are Egyptian. They are shown in purple.

Arabic Sounds Similar to English

ب	**b**	ن	**n**
ت	**t**	ه	**h**
د	**d**	ج	**j**
ر	**r**	ج (Egyptian)	**g** sounds like **g**oat
ز	**z**	ث	**th** sounds like **th**ree
س	**s**	ذ	**dh** sounds like **th**eir
ش	**sh**	ا	**aa** sounds like m**a**t
ف	**f**	و	**oo** sounds like p**oo**dle
ك	**k**	ي	**ee** sounds like pi**e**ce
ل	**l**	ي	**y** sounds like **y**es
م	**m**	و	**w** sounds like **w**ow

Arabic Sounds Not Similar to English

ح	**H**	sounds like **h** but from the throat
خ	**kh**	sounds like Lo**ch** Ness
ص	**S**	a deep **s** sound, close to **s**ummer
ض	**D**	a deep **d** sound, close to **d**uck
ط	**T**	a deep **t** sound, close to **t**ar
ظ	**DH**	a deep **dh** sound
غ	**gh**	**r** as in **F**rench, from back in the throat
ق	**q**	a deep **k** sound, close to **c**all

Other Pronunciation Rules

The hamza has no English letter. It is shown as an apostrophe ' .
It sounds like a stop made while holding the breath.

ع is the 'ayn, shown as a single quote mark ' . It is similar to the sound
of a gag.

There are no letters for short vowels in Arabic, but they are pronounced.

u	sounds like p**u**t
i	sounds like p**i**t
a	sounds like the beginning of **u**p

My Home
بيتي
(baytee)

window
شباك
(shibaak)

lamp
لمبة
(lambah)

bathroom
حمام
(Ham-maam)

bedroom
أوضة النوم
('uDit alnoom)

television
تلفزيون
(tilifizyoon)

cat
قطة
(qiT-Tah)

living room
الصالة
(iS-Saalah)

kitchen
مطبخ
(maTbakh)

sofa
كنبة
(kanabah)

chair
كرسي
(kursee)

table
ترابيزة
(taraabeezah)

In the Morning
في الصباح
(fiS-SabaaH)

dresser
تسريحة
(tasreeHah)

clock
ساعة
(saaʿah)

teddy bear
دبدوب
(dabdoob)

doll
عروسة
(ʿaroosah)

pillow
مخدة
(makhad-dah)

bed
سرير
(sireer)

blanket
بطانية
(baT-Taanee-yah)

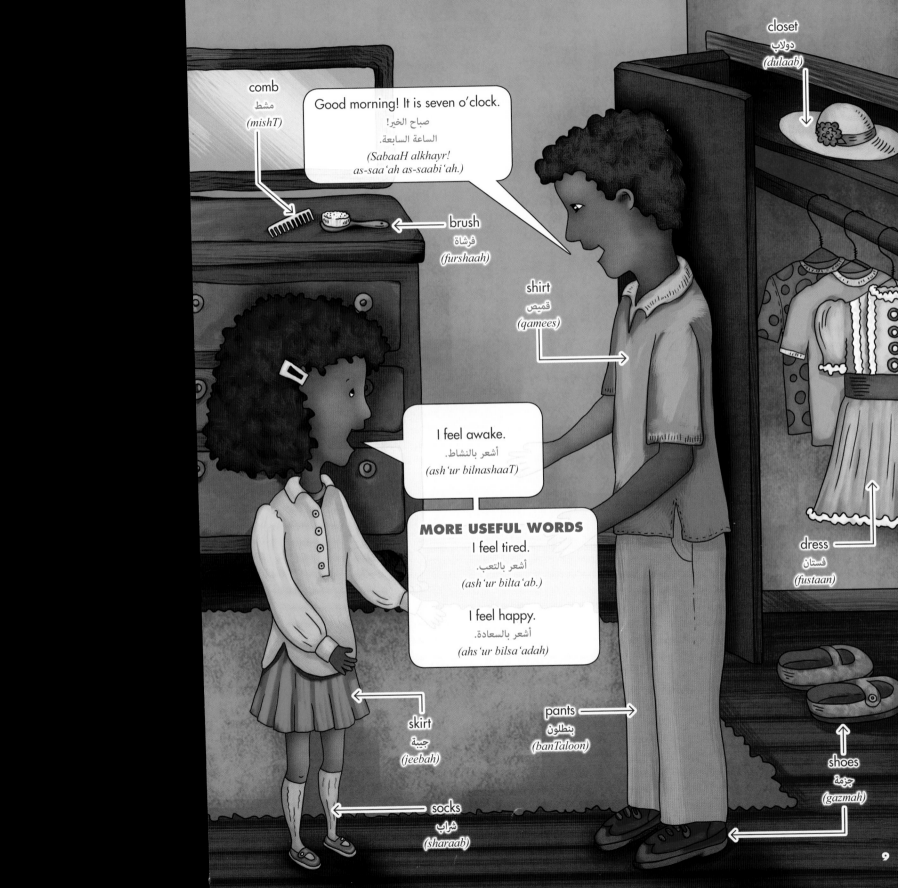

At the Park
في الجنينة
(fil gineenah)

Let's play!
يلا نلعب!
(yalla nil'ab)

sky
سماء
(samaa')

friend (male)
صديق
(Sadeeq)

friend (female)
صديقة
(Sadeeqah)

soccer ball
كرة القدم
(kurat alqadam)

bird
طائر
(Taa'ir)

MORE USEFUL WORDS

game
لعبة
(lu'bah)

sports
رياضات
(riyaaDaat)

sun
شمس
(shams)

swing
مرجيحة
(murgaiHah)

cloud
سحاب
(saHaab)

playground
ملعب
(mal'ab)

slide
زحليقة
(zuHleeqah)

water
ماء
(maa')

pond
بركة ماء
(birkat maa')

flower
زهرة
(zahrah)

duck
بطة
(baT-Tah)

13

Around Town
حول المدينة
(Hawla almadeenah)

library
مكتبة
(maktabah)

LIBRARY

firefighter
رجال إطفاء
(rajul 'Tfaa')

Excuse me.
عفوا.
('afwan)

woman
امرأة
(imraa'ah)

man
رجل
(rajul)

police officer
ضابط شرطة
(DaabiT shurTah)

street
شارع
(shaari')

airplane
طائرة
(Taa'irah)

office
مكتب
(maktab)

building
بناية
(binaayah)

OFFICE
BUILDING
2100

bus
أتوبيس
('utoobees)

CITY BUS

MORE USEFUL WORDS

truck
شاحنة
(shaaHinah)

train
قطار
(qiTaar)

stop
توقف
(tawaqaf)

go
تحرك
(taHarak)

15

My Birthday Party
حفلة عيد ميلادي
(Haflat 'eed meelaadee)

MORE USEFUL WORDS

one واحد *(waaHid)*	eleven أحد عشر *('aHad 'ashar)*
two اثنان *(ithnaan)*	twelve اثني عشر *(ithnaa 'ashar)*
three ثلاثة *(thalaathah)*	thirteen ثلاثة عشر *(thalathat 'ashar)*
four أربعة *(arba'ah)*	fourteen أربعة عشر *(arba'at 'ashar)*
five خمسة *(khamsah)*	fifteen خمسة عشر *(khamsat 'ashar)*
six ستة *(sit-tah)*	sixteen ستة عشر *(sitat 'ashar)*
seven سبعة *(sab'ah)*	seventeen سبعة عشر *(sab'at 'ashar)*
eight ثمانية *(thamaaniyah)*	eighteen ثمانية عشر *(thamaaniyat 'ashar)*
nine تسعة *(tis'ah)*	nineteen تسعة عشر *(tis'at 'ashar)*
ten عشرة *('asharah)*	twenty عشرون *('ishroon)*

grandmother
جدة
(jad-dah)

I am six years old.
أنا عمري ست سنوات.
(anaa 'umree sit sanwaat.)

grandfather
جد
(jadd)

brother
أخ
('akh)

sister
أخت
('ukht)

cake
كيكة
(kaykah)

19

At Night
في المساء
(fil masaa')

Good night! (male)
تصبح على خير!
(tusbiH 'alaa khayr!)

Good night! (female)
تصبحين على خير!
(tusbiHeen 'alaa khayr!)

MORE USEFUL WORDS

Today is Friday.
اليوم الجمعة.
(alyawm aljumu'ah)

Yesterday was Thursday.
أمس كان الخميس.
(ams kaan alkhamees)

Tomorrow is Saturday.
غدا السبت.
(ghadan as-sabt)

bathtub
بانيو
(banyoo)

I am tired!
أنا تعبان!
('anaa ta'baan)

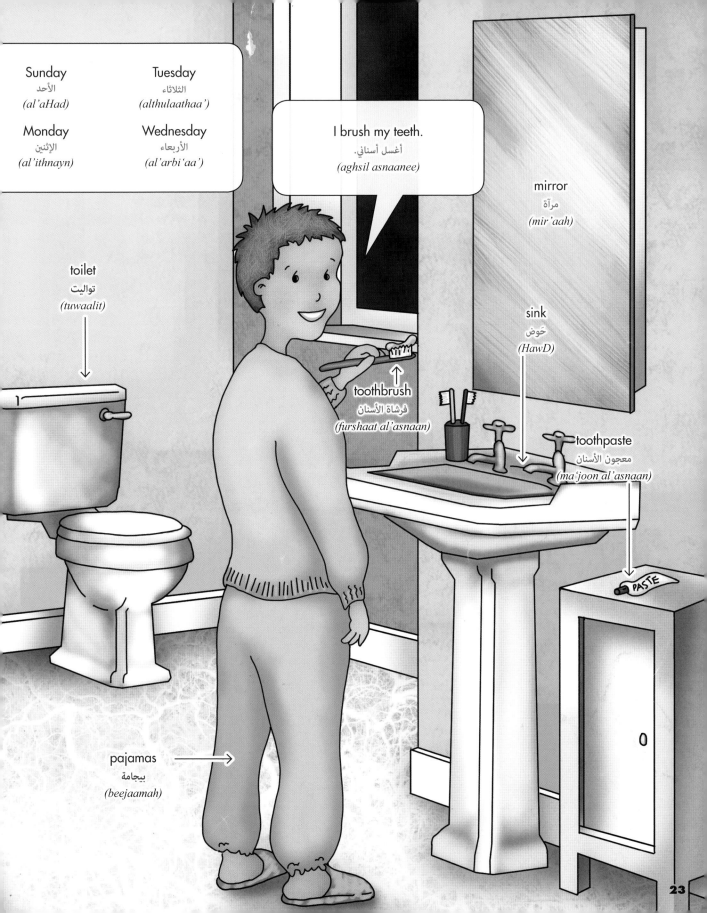

MORE USEFUL WORDS

Yes
نعم
(na'am)

No
لا
(laa)

ten
عشرة
('ashrah)

twenty
عشرون
('ishroon)

thirty
ثلاثون
(thalaathoon)

forty
أربعون
(arba'oon)

fifty
خمسون
(khamsoon)

sixty
ستون
(sit-toon)

seventy
سبعون
(sab'oon)

eighty
ثمانون
(thmanoon)

ninety
تسعون
(tis'oon)

one hundred
مئة
(mi'ah)

January
يناير
(yanaayir)

February
فبراير
(fibraayir)

March
مارس
(maaris)

April
أبريل
('abreel)

May
مايو
(mayoo)

June
يونيو
(yunyoo)

July
يوليو
(Yulyoo)

August
أغسطس
('ughusTus)

September
سبتمبر
(sibtambir)

October
اكتوبر
('uktubar)

November
نوفمبر
(noofamber)

December
ديسمبر
(deesambir)

winter
الشتاء
(ash-shitaa')

spring
الربيع
(ar-rabee')

summer
الصيف
(aS-Sayf)

fall
الخريف
(alkhareef)

good-bye!
وداعا!
(wada'an!)